The Kohlman Evaluation of Living Skills

Third Edition

by Linda Kohlman Thomson, MOT, OTR, OT(C), FAOTA

The American
Occupational Therapy
Association, Inc.

Disclaimers

"This publication is designed to provide accurate and authoritative information in regard to the subject matter covered. It is sold or distributed with the understanding that the publisher is not engaged in rendering legal, accounting, or other professional service. If legal advice or other expert assistance is required, the services of a competent professional person should be sought."
— From the Declaration of Principles jointly adopted by the American Bar Association and a Committee of Publishers and Associations.

It is the objective of the American Occupational Therapy Association to be a forum for free expression and interchange of ideas. The opinions and positions expressed by the contributors to this work are their own and not necessarily those of either the editors or the American Occupational Therapy Association.

Edited by John Hutchins
Designed by Robert Sacheli

Printed in the United States of America

ISBN 0-910317-90-9

Table of Contents

Acknowledgments and Preface

The development of the Kohlman Evaluation of Living Skills (KELS) has been a process that began in 1977 when I first started working as an occupational therapist on a locked inpatient psychiatric unit. Each edition has made it a more effective assessment tool. In the ongoing development of the KELS, more research is needed to further establish its reliability and validity. With such continued research and feedback from therapists, more improvements may be made in the future.

Many people have contributed to the success and acceptance of the KELS in the field of occupational therapy. I wish to acknowledge several special people. Trisha Thompson, MEd, OTR, developed a living skills evaluation that preceded the KELS. Appreciation is also expressed to Michal Sheffer, PhD, OTR, who helped me establish my interest and foundation in psychiatric occupational therapy. I also wish to thank Michal for the encouragement and suggestions she gave me in the initial stages of development of the KELS. Susan Kronsnoble, OTR, has helped in many ways with continual support, feedback, and assistance with research. Her help has been invaluable. A special thank-you is given to the investigators who chose to do research on the KELS. Their work has contributed significantly to the refinement of the KELS and to the establishment of its reliability and validity. I must also thank the many occupational therapists who have worked with me in a variety of settings and provided me with feedback and positive reinforcement. There are also the many occupational therapists across the country who have been willing to provide me with similar feedback and encouragement. All this help has made it possible for me to be able to continue working on the KELS. Thank you all for your assistance. Please continue to help with your feedback and encouragement.

Linda Kohlman Thomson, MOT, OTR, OT(C), FAOTA

Introduction

The Kohlman Evaluation of Living Skills (KELS) is an occupational therapy evaluation that is designed to determine a person's ability to function in basic living skills. The administration of the evaluation combines interview questions and tasks. The KELS is easy to learn and can be administered and scored in a short period of time—usually in 30 to 45 minutes. The equipment required can be assembled easily by the occupational therapist and transported with little effort. The Score Sheet is easy to read and communicates the results of the evaluation effectively (see Appendix K). Using the results, the therapist makes recommendations for living situations that allow clients to function as independently as possible. Seventeen living skills are tested under five areas: Self-Care, Safety and Health, Money Management, Transportation and Telephone, and Work and Leisure (see Score Sheet in Appendix I).

The goal of the Kohlman Evaluation of Living Skills is the successful integration of an individual into his or her environment. The inability to perform daily living skills is often a factor that causes people to seek treatment. The KELS helps identify the areas in which a person can perform and those in which the person needs assistance. R. W. White (1959), in an article about motivation, discussed the intrinsic need for individuals to deal with the environment. White said that if a person can interact effectively with the environment, then his or her sense of competency and satisfaction are increased. Motivation involves the satisfaction that occurs in successful experiences with the environment. Activities of daily living are all ways in which individuals interact and control the environment. The KELS helps to match people with environments in which success can be experienced, thereby increasing satisfaction and motivation. Satisfaction, motivation, and independence in the environment are all factors of health for an individual.

The KELS was originally created for use in a short-term inpatient psychiatric unit. With the many changes in the delivery of health care services and the aging of the population, the applicability of the KELS in other intervention settings has grown dramatically. It is an excellent tool for use with the elderly because it assists team and family members to help a person live as independently as possible and yet be safe. Occupational therapists may also use the KELS in acute care hospitals where they are frequently asked to assist in discharge planning but are given very little time to provide the appropriate information. By using the easily administered KELS, an occupational therapist is able to assist the team quickly with discharge planning.

In some states, the KELS is used in court for the determination of commitment and gravely disabled cases. The KELS is also an appropriate evaluation for individuals who have cognitively disabling conditions, such as organic brain syndrome or Alzheimer disease, or who have been brain-injured in an accident. In settings with long lengths of stays, the KELS may not be the best living skill assessment to use because the person's financial, transportation, work, and leisure resources have usually changed dramatically due to the long length of stay at the facility (see Applications and Limitations section).

In the Administration section, the necessary equipment, the administration procedures, and the scoring criteria for each item are given. Sections on Equipment and Scoring provide more detailed information required for administering the KELS. The Research section describes studies that demonstrate the effectiveness of the KELS. Examples of completed KELS Score Sheets are located in Appendix K.

The Kohlman Evaluation of Living Skills is a tool for use in the assessment process to determine the levels of independence of a person and to make recommendations for appropriate living situations. Although the KELS is not a comprehensive evaluation, it quickly provides information about the ability of a person to function in basic living skills.

Equipment

All of the equipment and forms necessary to administer the KELS can be assembled in approximately 1–1 $\frac{1}{2}$ hours. It is helpful to organize the equipment and forms in a three-ring binder. Zippered plastic cases and dividers with pockets can be used to store the equipment and forms in the order they are used. Whenever the KELS is administered, the occupational therapist only needs to pick up the notebook and local phone book(s) and have a telephone accessible in order to administer the evaluation.

The list below includes the equipment and forms needed to administer the Kohlman Evaluation of Living Skills. The forms that appear in the Appendices (pp. 55-67) may be photocopied for use in administering the KELS only.

Reading and Writing Form — See Appendix A to copy form.

Pencil

Household Situation Pictures (4) — The four pictures are located in Appendix B.

Phone Book(s) — Use the local white and yellow page telephone book(s). If the client's local telephone book(s) are not available, use the telephone book(s) from the locality in which the evaluation is being administered.

Deck of Cards — Copy the $1.58 price tag from Appendix C and tape it on a deck of cards. An example is given in Appendix C. Do not substitute another price, because the prices have been carefully selected in order for the client to use specific money and math skills. You may substitute another item for the deck of cards if necessary, but use only an item that is small, appropriate for the price, universally used, and not biased by gender in its use.

Bar of Soap — Copy the $.23 price tag from Appendix C and tape it on a bar of soap. An example is given in Appendix C. Do not substitute another price, because the prices have been carefully selected in order for the client to use specific money and math skills. You may substitute another item for the bar of soap if necessary, but only use an item that is small, appropriate for the price, universally used, and not biased by gender in its use.

Two (2) One Dollar Bills

One (1) Half Dollar

Two (2) Quarters

One (1) Dime

Four (4) Pennies

Budget Form — See Appendix D to copy form.

Checking Account Form — See Appendix E to copy forms or obtain blank check forms and check registers from a local bank. Many banks have practice checking account forms available. If local bank forms are unavailable, copy the form in Appendix E and cut it down to actual size. If actual banking forms are used, write in $46.00 for the balance on the check register as it is shown on the form in Appendix E. Do not change the balance or the task will be invalid and unreliable.

Savings Account Form — See Appendix F to copy form or obtain blank savings withdrawal forms from a local bank. If local bank forms are unavailable, copy the form in Appendix F and cut it down to the actual size.

Bill — See Appendix G for a sample bill. Obtain a local electricity bill and remove the name, address, and due date. Copy the bill and cut it down to the actual size. Write in a due date one to two months ahead of the date the KELS is administered. This date will need to be changed regularly.

Taxi Company Card — See Appendix H for an example. Select a taxi company from the local telephone book. Make sure the telephone number is located in both the yellow and white pages. Print or type the name of the taxi company in large letters and mount it on a sturdy card.

Connected Telephone

Recorded Message Card — See Appendix H for an example. Select a telephone number with a recorded message. Make sure there is no charge for the call. Movie theater telephone numbers that provide recorded movie show times work well for this task. Print or type the name of the business and the telephone number in large block print and mount it on a sturdy card.

Score Sheet — See Appendix I. This form can be copied onto standard progress note paper to be used in a client's chart or record.

Administration

E ach living skill evaluation item is divided into four sections: the method (task or interview), the equipment, the administration procedures, and the scoring criteria. Specific instructions and questions to be asked by the evaluator are printed in boldface, italic letters. State these as given, because if an item is not administered correctly and as stated, the established reliability and validity of the KELS will not be applicable.

Be brief in your questioning. Stay on the subject and limit conversation to the item you are evaluating. Additional comments should be avoided unless they are needed to maintain the attention of the client.*

During the administration of the evaluation, do not give feedback concerning the scores you are giving the client. If the client specifically asks or is unusually anxious about the results, restate that you will go over the results after completing the evaluation.

The client should sit to the left of the evaluator (reverse if the evaluator is left-handed) or across the table. This will allow the evaluator to write notes or score the KELS without the score sheet being between the client and the evaluator and creating a distraction.

Use a three-ring binder to hold the KELS manual, forms, and supplies. Dividers with pockets can be used to hold the forms and zippered plastic cases can hold the necessary equipment. Further instructions for creating a KELS notebook are included in the Equipment section (p. 9).

Before administering the KELS, the evaluator should determine the location of the client's residence and whether the client has been living alone or with other people. This information will assist the evaluator in determining the accuracy of the answers and the applicability of some items for that client.

---

*The term *client*, used throughout the text, refers to any individual to whom the KELS is given, including patients and residents of institutions.

Introduction

Evaluator:

- *I will be giving you an evaluation of living skills. The reason I am giving you this evaluation is to help determine your specific skills and to assist in intervention and discharge planning. It will take approximately 20-30 minutes to administer. I may be writing down notes as the evaluation progresses. If you have any questions, feel free to stop me at any time. At the end of the evaluation* [or at another designated time], *I will go over the results with you. Are you ready to begin?*

Reading and Writing

This section is used to obtain information that is supplemental to the actual evaluation. While it is not used to determine if the client can live independently, it can provide the evaluator with valuable information about the client's level of cognitive function (orientation and memory) and reading and writing skills. It also gives the evaluator information that is used to score the *Frequency of self-care activities* item (p. 15), which is scored later in the evaluation.

Method
Task

Equipment
Reading and Writing Form
Pencil

Administration
Place the Reading and Writing Form and a pencil in front of the client.

Instructions:
• *First, do this.*

(Don't say, "fill this in." The client needs to read and comprehend the directions as independently as possible).

Self-Care
1. Appearance

The client must be in street clothes to score this item. If he or she is not dressed in street clothes, note this at the side of the item on the Score Sheet and write "See Note" in the scoring boxes (see Appendix K – Sample Score Sheet #1).

Method   Observation

Scoring   **Independent**: No more than one of the conditions listed under "Needs Assistance" is present.

Needs Assistance: At least two of the conditions listed below are present.
  hair dirty and/or uncombed
  ragged and/or torn clothing
  clothing not fastened properly
  unpleasant body odor
  dirty fingernails and/or ungroomed hands
  visible dirt on body
  dirty clothing
  obvious dental decay
  open untreated sores

Self-Care

2. Frequency of self-care activities (self-report)

Method	Task and/or Interview
Equipment	Reading and Writing Form Pencil
Administration	The client fills in the bottom of the Reading and Writing Form. When the form is finished, quickly review the answers to see that each response is complete. If a response is not complete, ask the client questions until you understand each answer.
Alternate Administration Method	If the client is unable to complete the form, use interview questions phrased in this manner: • *How often do you take a shower or bath?* • *How often do you wash your face?* Proceed down the Reading and Writing Form and fill in the responses for the client.

Scoring	**Independent**: The client's frequency of self-care activities is equal to or greater than the minimum standards listed below.
	
	Needs Assistance: The client's frequency of one or more of the self-care activities is less than the minimum standards listed below.
	
	Minimum Standards for Frequency of Self-Care Activities
	    Shower or Bathe: *once a week*
	    Wash Face: *once a day*
	    Wash Hair: *once a week*
	    Comb Hair: *once a day*
	    Brush Teeth: *once a day*
	    Eat: *twice a day*

Safety and Health

1. Awareness of dangerous household situations (from photographs)

Method	Task
Equipment	Four (4) Household Situation Pictures **Note**: The pictures have been carefully selected and tested to evaluate different dangerous situations in the home. They were selected based on data from accidents in the home. Some of the photographs are purposely dark so that the client must demonstrate the ability to use figure ground and visual skills.

Administration	Give the following introduction:
	• *I am going to show you four pictures. There may be a dangerous situation in them, or there may not be anything dangerous at all. Look carefully at each of them. You must decide if there is anything dangerous in the pictures.*
	
	Present the Household Situation Pictures in the following order:
	    Picture 1. Cord across the hallway
	    Picture 2. Standing on the phone book
	    Picture 3. Safe picture
	    Picture 4. Hair dryer by sink
	
	Show each picture to the client and ask:
	• *Do you see anything dangerous in this picture?*
	
	If the client answers "No," proceed to the next picture.
	
	If the client answers "Yes," ask:
	• *What is dangerous?*
	
	If the client only gives a partial answer and has not specifically identified the dangerous element and what is dangerous about it, ask:
	• *What is dangerous about* [use client's partial answer]*?*
	Examples:
	• *What is dangerous about the cord?*
	• *What is dangerous about the light fixture?*

Scoring	**Independent**: The client must identify both the dangerous element (if one is present in the picture) and why it is dangerous. Both components must be

present in the client's response. The client must give the following responses:

Picture 1: Yes. The cord is across the doorway, and someone could trip.

Picture 2: Yes. The phone book is an unstable surface to climb on, and he could fall.

Picture 3. No dangerous element present.

Picture 4. Yes. The hair dryer is near water, and someone could get shocked.

Needs Assistance: The client gives one or more incorrect answers.

Safety and Health

2. Identification of appropriate action for sickness and accidents

Method	Interview
Equipment	Phone Book(s)
Administration	Ask the following questions:

1. *What would you do for yourself if you got sick with a cold?*
2. *What would you do if you burned yourself and the wound became infected?*
3. *What would you do if you suddenly started having severe chest pains and shortness of breath?*

If the client only gives a partial answer, ask further questions until you are satisfied that the client has given you his or her complete knowledge. Ask who, what, where, and how questions.
Examples:
1. If only a partial answer is given, ask:
   - *Would you do anything else?*
2. If the client responds, "I'd get help," ask:
   - *How would you get help?*
3. If the client responds that he or she would call the local emergency number, but doesn't give the actual number, ask:
   - *What is the telephone number you would use?*
   The client may use the phone book if needed.

Scoring

Independent: The client must answer all three questions as listed below.
1. The client gives at least one of the items listed below:
   - take aspirin or cold pills
   - drink fluids
   - rest
   - go to the doctor

2. The client would go to the doctor.

3. The client would get help by calling the local emergency number (must state actual number) or the operator. If the client uses the phone book and locates the number in the phone book without assistance, mark as "Independent."

Needs Assistance: If one or more questions are not answered as given above.

Safety and Health
3. Knowledge of emergency numbers

Method	Interview and/or Task
Equipment	Phone Book(s)
Administration	**For localities with a single emergency number:**

For localities with a single emergency number:
If the client has given the local emergency number as part of an answer to Safety and Health, Section #2 (p. 18), score as "Independent" and go on to the next item.

If the local emergency number has not been given, ask:
- *In an emergency, what telephone number would you call?*

If the client responds, "I'd look it up in the phone book," hand the phone book(s) to the client and state:
- *Find the number you would use in the phone book.*

If the client does not mention using the phone book, do not hand it to the client.

For localities with separate emergency numbers for different types of emergencies:
If the client has given the local emergency numbers that would contact the police, fire department, and/or aid car (or ambulance) as part of an answer in Safety and Health, Section #2 (p. 18), score as "Independent" and go on to the next item.

If the emergency numbers have not been given, ask:
- *If you needed the police in an emergency, what telephone number would you call?*

- *If you needed the fire department in an emergency, what telephone number would you call?*

- *If you needed an aid car or an ambulance in an emergency, what telephone number would you call?*

If the client responds, "I'd look it up in the phone book," hand the phone book(s) to the client and state:
- *Find the number you would use in the phone book.*

If the client does not mention using the phone book, do not hand it to the client.

<table>
<tr><td>Scoring</td><td>Independent: The client gives the local emergency number(s) or the operator's number. The actual number(s) must be given.

The client mentions using a phone book and then proceeds to locate the number(s) in the phone book without assistance.

Needs Assistance: The client does not give the local emergency number(s) or the number of the operator.

The client looks in the phone book for the emergency number(s) but does not find the number(s) without help from the evaluator.</td></tr>
</table>

Safety and Health
4. Knowledge of location of medical and dental facilities

Method	Interview and/or Task
Equipment	Phone Book(s)
Administration	Ask:

Method Interview and/or Task

Equipment Phone Book(s)

Administration Ask:
- *If you needed to see a doctor, where would you go?*

If the client only gives a name and not the location, ask:
- *Where is Dr.* [doctor's name]*'s office located?*

Ask:
- *If you needed to see a dentist, where would you go?*

If the client only gives a name and not the location, ask:
- *Where is Dr.* [dentist's name]*'s office located?*

For either question, if the client responds, "I'd look it up in the phone book," hand the phone book(s) to the client and ask:
- *Find Dr.* [doctor's or dentist's name] *in the phone book.*

Scoring **Independent**: Check the addresses to determine the accuracy of the answers given. For each question, client gives one or more of the responses listed below:
- name of doctor and dentist and where the offices are located (general vicinity is acceptable)
- name of hospital and where it is located (general vicinity is acceptable)
- name of clinic or special program that provides medical/dental services and where it is located (general vicinity is acceptable)

If the client mentions using the phone book and then proceeds to locate the Physician or Dentist section in the phone book or a specific address without assistance, mark as "Independent."

Needs Assistance: The client does not give at least one of the responses listed under "Independent" for each question.

If the client looks in the phone book for a location, but does not find the Physician or Dentist section in the phone book or a specific address without help from the evaluator, score as "Needs Assistance."

Money Management
1. Use of money in purchasing items

Method	Task
Equipment	Deck of cards with $1.58 price tag Bar of soap with $.23 price tag Two (2) - one dollar bills One (1) - half dollar Two (2) - quarters One (1) - dime Four (4) - pennies

Note: The prices, coins, and tasks have been carefully selected so that the client will have to use specific money and math skills. Do not change the prices, coins, or tasks. If necessary, you may substitute another item for the deck of cards or the bar of soap, but use only an item that is small, appropriate for the price, universally used, and not biased by gender in its use. If an item is substituted, continue to use the price tags of $1.58 and $.23.

Administration

Task One
State the following instructions:
- *I'm going to give you two dollars, and you're going to buy this deck of cards from me. The deck of cards costs $1.58, including tax* [point to price tag]. *You give me the two dollars, and I give you the deck of cards and this amount of change* [hand client $.37 in change — 1 quarter, 1 dime, and 2 pennies]. *Is that the right amount of change?*

If client answers "Yes," proceed to the Task Two.

If the client answers "No," ask:
- *What would be the right amount?*

Task Two
State the following instructions:
- *Now I'm going to give you one dollar, and you're going to buy this bar of soap from me. The bar of soap costs $.23, including tax* [point to price tag]. *You give me the dollar, and I give you the bar of soap and this amount of change* [hand the client $.77 in change — 1 half dollar, 1 quarter, and 2 pennies]. *Is that the right amount of change?*

If the client answers "No," ask:
- *What would be the right amount?*

Scoring

Independent: The client completes both tasks correctly without using paper to figure the answers.

Correct answers:

    Task One: No. Indicates or states $.42. It is also correct if the client responds that the evaluator gave a nickel less than the correct amount.

    Task Two: Yes.

Needs Assistance: The client completes one or both tasks incorrectly. Score as "Needs Assistance" if the client uses paper to figure the answers.

Money Management
2. Obtain and maintain source of income

Method	Interview
Equipment	Phone Book(s)
Administration	Ask:

Ask:
- *What is your source of income?*

If the client doesn't understand, ask:
- *Where do you get your money?*

Note: It is helpful to make a note at the side of the item of the Score Sheet identifying the source of income (see Appendix K – Sample Score Sheet #2).

1. If the client responds "from public assistance" and/or "from Social Security Insurance [SSI]," ask:
- *If your check didn't come one month, what would you do to find out what happened to it?*

  If the client does not say a specific office, ask:
  - *What office do you use?*
  The client may use the phone book, if needed.

2. If the client responds "from work," ask:
- *Where do you work?*

  A. If the client gives a place of employment, ask:
  - *Do you plan on returning to work there?*

    If the client responds "Yes," ask:
    - *When do you plan on returning to work?*
    Stop here and proceed to next item.

    If the client responds "No," ask:
    - *Do you plan on getting another job?*

      If the client responds "Yes," ask:
      - *When do you plan on getting another job?*
      Stop here and proceed to next item.

      If the client responds "No," ask:
      - *What will be your source of income?*
      Stop here and proceed to next item.

B. If the client responds that he or she does not presently have a job, ask:
- *Do you plan on getting another job?*

    If the client responds "Yes," ask:
    - *When do you plan on getting another job?*
    Stop here and proceed to next item.

    If the client responds "No," ask:
    - *What will be your source of income?*
    Stop here and proceed to next item.

3. If the client responds that he or she has no income or that income is provided by another person, stop here and proceed to next item. Examples:
    1. Spouse or significant other provides the income.
    2. An adolescent who has never lived away from home and whose parents provide all of his or her income and daily expenses.

Scoring

If the client responds "from public assistance and/or SSI," use the scoring categories listed below:

Independent: Client says that he or she would call or visit a specific public assistance and/or SSI office. Check a listing of local offices to see if the client has the location correct. The client needs to know where an office is located or be able to find one independently in the phone book.

Needs Assistance: Client does not know what to do or does not know a specific office.

If the client responds "from work," use the scoring categories listed below:

Independent: Either condition listed below:
1. Client has a job and plans to return to work within a month.
2. Client does not have a job but has realistic plans to get a job within a month.

Needs Assistance: Employment does not seem reasonable for this client, or the client will be unemployed for longer than one month after discharge with no other source of income identified. Score either condition as "Needs Assistance."

If the client responds "no income," score as "Needs Assistance."

Money Management

3. Budgeting of money for food

If the client does not manage his or her money independently, score as "Needs Assistance" and do not administer this item. For example, the client may be living in a setting where a room and board charge includes the provision of food, or a parent, family member, or friend may provide and budget for food (see Appendix K – Sample Score Sheet #2).

Method

Interview

Administration

Ask:

• *How much money do you spend a month for food for yourself?*
Make sure the response does not include money spent for food for other people.

Scoring

Independent: The client spends in either cash or food stamps at least the amount allotted per month by the United States government Food Stamp Program for one person with no income ($111.00 per month as of October 1, 1992).*

Needs Assistance: The client spends in cash or food stamps less than the amount allotted per month by the United States government Food Stamp Program for one person with no income ($111.00 per month as of October 1, 1992)* or is unable to give an amount of money spent for food.

---

* This amount is updated every October 1 by the Food Stamp Program. The current figure is available from state departments of social and/or health services or the US Department of Agriculture (Food and Nutrition Service). Contact numbers for these institutions are listed in local telephone books.

Money Management
4. Budgeting of monthly income

If a spouse, significant other, or halfway house handles the budgeting for the client, score as "Needs Assistance" and do not administer this item. Note who does the budgeting on the Score Sheet (see Appendix K – Sample Score Sheet #2).

Method	Task and/or Interview
Equipment	Budget Form Pencil
Administration	Ask: • *What is your monthly income?* Place the Budget Form and a pencil in front of the client. Instructions: • *Fill in this form by listing how much money you spend for the following categories each month.* If the client is unable to complete the form, use the interview questions listed below: • *How much money do you spend for rent?* • *How much money do you spend for utilities?* Proceed down the form and fill in the client's responses for each category. If the client gives a different figure for food than was given for the previous item (p. 26), clarify which figure is correct and score the items accordingly.
Scoring	**Independent**: The client gives figures for at least three categories. The total of the figures must be no greater than the client's monthly income and no less than 90% of the client's monthly income. Example: If the monthly income is $500, then the total must be within the range of $450 to $500. **Needs Assistance**: The client gives figures for less than three categories. The total of the figures is greater than the client's monthly income or less than 90% of the client's monthly income. Either condition is scored as "Needs Assistance."

Money Management
5. Use of banking forms

Method	Task and Interview
Equipment	Checking Account Form Savings Account Form Pencil
Administration	If the client responds "Yes" to a question, proceed to the indicated task and omit the further interview questions. If the client answers "No" to all four interview questions, mark "Not Applicable" in the Scoring Boxes for this item on the Score Sheet (see Appendix K – Sample Score Sheet #1).

Depending on the client's answers, either one task or no task will be administered. Do not administer both the Checking Account Task and the Savings Account Task.

Ask:

1. ***Do you have a checking account now?***
   If the client responds "Yes," proceed to the Checking Account Task given below and do not ask any further interview questions.

   If the client responds "No," ask the next question.

2. ***Do you have a savings account now?***
   If the client responds "Yes," proceed to the Savings Account Task given below and do not ask any further interview questions.

   If the client responds "No," ask the next interview question.

3. ***Have you ever had a checking account?***
   If the client responds "Yes," proceed to the Checking Account Task given below and do not ask any further interview questions.

   If the client responds "No," ask the next interview question.

4. ***Have you ever had a savings account?***
   If the client responds "Yes," proceed to the Savings Account Task given below.

   If the client responds "No" to all four questions, mark "Not Applicable" in the Scoring Boxes for this item on the Score Sheet (see Appendix K – Sample Score Sheet #1).

Checking Account Task

Hand the client the Checking Account Form and a pencil. Instructions:

* ***Make out this check to Safeway for $17.88.***

After the client finishes the first part, say:

* ***Record it in the proper place.***

Repeat the instructions if needed.

Savings Account Task

Hand the client the Savings Account Form and a pencil. Instructions:

* ***Using this form, withdraw $20.00 from your savings account.***

Repeat the instructions if needed.

Scoring

For the Checking Account Form:

Independent: The client fills out the check, records it, and subtracts the amount from the register total. All sections are completed accurately. Refer to the sample completed form on the next page.

Needs Assistance: Client does not complete all three steps or makes errors in the process.

For the Savings Account Form:

Independent: The client fills out the Savings Account Form completely and accurately. Refer to the sample completed form on the next page.

Needs Assistance: The client does not complete the form or makes errors in the process.

Checking Account Sample Form

Check No.	Date	Checks drawn or deposits made	Amount of check (−)	Check fee (if any)	Amount of deposit (+)	BALANCE FORWARD $ 46.00	✓
105	3/23	Safeway	$17.88			17.88	
						28.12	

Please be sure to deduct any per check charges or maintenance charges that may apply to your account

1st National Bank
105

NON-NEGOTIABLE
PRACTICE CHECK

March 23 19 92

PAY TO
THE ORDER OF Safeway $ 17.88

Seventeen and 88/100 _____ DOLLARS

MEMO _____   Sarah Townes

Savings Account Sample Form

☐ SEND CASHIER'S CHECK
☐ DEPOSIT TO CHECKING ACCOUNT

DATE March 23, 1992

CHARGE MY
SAVINGS
ACCOUNT twenty and 20/100 _____ DOLLARS

SAVINGS WITHDRAWAL

AMOUNT WITHDRAWN	
$ 20	00

SIGNATURE Sarah Townes

Money Management
6. Payment of bills

Method	Task
Equipment	Bill with current due date written in.
Administration	Hand the bill to the client. Instructions: 1. ***What is the amount due on this bill?*** 2. ***When is this bill due?*** 3. ***How would you pay this bill?***

Scoring	**Independent**: All three answers must be correct. Client answers:
	1. Amount due is $43.11 or amount on a local bill.
	2. Current due date on bill.
	3. Can pay in one of two ways:
	  • mail to City Electric Company
	  • pay in person at City Electric Company office
	These methods of payment need to be adjusted according to how utility bills are paid in the client's home area.
	
	Needs Assistance: If any of the conditions listed below are present:
	1. Client does not give the correct amount due on the bill.
	2. Client does not give the correct due date on the bill.
	3. Client does not give one of the methods to pay the bill listed under "Independent." Remember to consider the methods by which utility bills may be paid in the client's home area.

Transportation and Telephone
1. Mobility within community

Method	Interview
Administration	Ask: • *How do you get from one place to another in* [name of the city the client lives in]*?* If the client only mentions walking, ask: • *Do you use any other means of transportation?* For each method of transportation stated by client, ask: • *When was the last time you* [method of transportation given]*?*
Scoring	Next to the item on the Score Sheet, make a note of the transportation methods used by the client (see Appendix K for Sample Score Sheets). **Independent**: Both of the conditions listed below must be present: 1. The client gives at least one method of transportation (besides walking) that can be done without any participation by another individual and does not require another person's property (i.e., car or bicycle). Using taxis, public transportation, and the client's own bicycle are acceptable. Examples not acceptable for scoring "Independent" are driving a parent's car or having a friend provide transportation. 2. At least one method of transportation (besides walking) has been used within the past month. **Needs Assistance**: The client only uses walking for transportation, does not leave the house, or all methods require the participation of another individual or another person's property. The client has not used a transportation method (besides walking) in the past month, or the methods stated would not enable the client to meet necessary daily living needs independently.

Transportation and Telephone
2. Basic knowledge of transit system

This item is designed for clients who live in cities with public transit systems. If the client's city does not have a public transit system, mark "Not Applicable" in the scoring boxes for this item.

Method

Interview

Adminstration

Ask:

- *If you needed to take a bus to a place you hadn't been before, how would you know what bus to ride?*

Scoring

Independent: The client gives at least one of the answers listed below. (Transit systems in different localities may affect the acceptability of these answers.)

1. Gives the number of the bus route closest to where the client lives (check if necessary).
2. Asks the bus driver.
3. Reads bus stop signs.
4. Calls transit information number.
5. Reads bus schedule.

Needs Assistance: The client does not know how to find out what bus to ride or gives an answer that would not enable the client to take the correct bus.

Transportation and Telephone
3. Use of phone book and telephone

Method	Task
Equipment	Phone Book(s) Taxi Company Card Connected Telephone Recorded Message Card
Administration	Place the phone book(s) in front of the client. Ask: • *What is the telephone number for directory assistance or information? You may use the phone book if you wish.* Place the taxi company card in front of the client. Instructions: • *Find the telephone number for* [name of taxi company]. Place the connected telephone in front of the client or take the client to a telephone. (If a telephone is not convenient, save this item until the end of the evaluation when you can take the client to a telephone.) Place the recorded message card in front of the client. Instructions: • *Here is the telephone number for* [name of recorded message]. *Call the number and tell me the* [information from the recorded message]. Example: Here is the telephone number for the IMAX Theater. Call the number and tell me the time the first movie will be shown.
Scoring	**Independent**: All conditions listed below must be present: 1. The client gives or is able to locate the number for directory assistance or information independently. It is also acceptable if the client would call the operator or dial 0. 2. The client independently locates the number for the taxi company in either the white or yellow pages. 3. The client dials the telephone number for the recorded message accurately without assistance and reports the correct information from the message. **Needs Assistance**: Any of the conditions listed below are present: 1. The client does not give the telephone numbers for directory assistance or information. 2. The client cannot locate telephone number(s) for directory assistance,

information, or the taxi company without assistance from the evaluator.
3. The client cannot dial the telephone accurately and report the correct information from the recorded message.

Work and Leisure
1. Plans for future employment

Method	Interview
Administration	Determine the client's employment status from the item *Obtain and maintain source of income* (p. 24). Using this information, select the appropriate employment situation below and proceed with the interview.

1. Client is presently employed and plans to return to the same job.
Score as "Independent" and do not administer this item (see Appendix K – Sample Score Sheet #3).

2. Client has worked in the past, is presently unemployed, but plans to work in the future. Ask:
- *When was your last job?*
- *What kind of job was it?*
- *What kind of a job will you look for in the future?*
- *How will you find a job?*

3. Client has worked in the past, is presently unemployed, and doesn't plan to work in the future.
Mark "See Note" in the scoring boxes for the item and write a short note next to the item on the Score Sheet indicating that the client has worked but doesn't plan to work in the future (see Appendix K – Sample Score Sheet #1).

4. Client is on public assistance or SSI. Ask:
- *Have you worked in the past?*

If the client answers "Yes," ask:
- *Do you plan on working in the future?*

If the client answers "Yes," ask:
- *When was your last job?*
- *What kind of job was it?*
- *What kind of job will you look for in the future?*
- *How will you find a job?*

If the client answers "No," mark "See Note" in the scoring boxes and write a short note to the side of the item on the Score Sheet indicating that the client has worked but doesn't plan to work in the future (see Appendix K – Sample Score Sheet #1).

If the client answers "No," ask:
- *Do you plan on working in the future?*

If the client answers "Yes," ask:
- *What kind of a job will you look for in the future?*
- *How will you find a job?*

If the client answers "No," mark "See Note" in the scoring boxes and write a short note to the side of the item on the Score Sheet indicating that the client has never worked and does not plan to work (see Appendix K – Sample Score Sheet #2).

5. Client is retired and doesn't plan to work in the future.
Mark "Not Applicable" in the scoring boxes for the item and write a short note next to the item on the Score Sheet indicating that the client is retired.

Scoring

If the client is presently employed and plans to return to the same job, score "Independent" for this item.

Independent: Both conditions listed below must be present:
1. The client plans to find a job by one of the methods below:
- Newspaper
- Signs in windows
- Relatives or friends who have jobs to offer
- Employment office
2. The kind of job given by the client matches the education, skills, and past history of the client. This is determined by observations and information gained from the client, the chart, or others. It must be reasonable for the client to pursue the kind of job given.

Needs Assistance: Any condition listed below:
1. The client's plans are not realistic in terms of the past history, education, and skills of the client.
2. The client does not know how to find a job or does not give one of the methods of finding a job listed under "Independent."

Work and Leisure

2. Leisure activity involvement

Method	Interview
Administration	Ask: • *What do you do in your leisure or free time?* If the client does not voluntarily give three leisure activities,* ask: • *Do you do anything else?* If the client does not voluntarily give any leisure activities done with other people, ask: • *Do you do any activities with other people?* After the client has responded to the above questions, ask for each activity given: • *When was the last time you* [state a leisure activity given by the client]*?* Repeat the question for each activity given by the client.
Scoring	**Independent**: Both of the conditions listed below must be present: 1. The client must give a minimum of three leisure activities, one of which is done with other people. 2. A minimum of three leisure activities must have been done within the previous month. One of these three must have been done with other people. **Needs Assistance**: Any of the conditions listed below are present: 1. The client gives less than three leisure activities. 2. No leisure activities are done with other people. 3. Less than three leisure activities were done within the previous month. 4. No leisure activity was done with other people within the previous month.

---

* Leisure activities: time spent free from the demands of work or duty; voluntary participation in activities with no obligation or responsibility to participate.

Scoring

There are two scoring categories for the KELS — "Independent" and "Needs Assistance." The specific criteria for determining the client's scores on each separate item appears at the end of the administration procedure for each item. The scoring criteria are based on the minimum standards required to live independently in the community. "Independent" is defined as the level of competency required to perform the basic living skills in a manner that maintains the safety and health of the individual without the direct assistance of other people.

The score of a "Needs Assistance" should not be viewed as being abnormal or negative in connotation. It is important to remember that many people require assistance for some of their daily living skills. If a person scores "Needs Assistance" on one item, it does not mean that the person is incapable of living independently. The score applies to that particular item, meaning, for that living skill, the person needs assistance. For instance, a homemaker whose husband manages the couple's money would probably score "Needs Assistance" for the items *Obtain and maintain source of income* (p. 24) and *Budgeting of monthly income* (p. 27). The homemaker may function independently overall, but, at present and in her current living situation, she needs assistance in those areas of daily living skills. In a different setting and social environment, the homemaker may be independent in those areas. The level of independence is determined by an overall score, as explained below, and not by individual items.

After the evaluator determines the score for an item, it is recommended that the appropriate scoring box on the Score Sheet be blackened in completely. This may take slightly longer than making a check mark or an X, but the mark is much more visible and enables other health care professionals to focus quickly and easily on the results (see Appendix K for Sample Score Sheets).

For special situations, the terms "Not Applicable" and "See Note" are used, but these terms should be used as infrequently as possible. "Not Applicable" is used for the items that do not pertain to the client's specific living situation (see Appendix K – Sample Score Sheets #1 and #3). For example, the item *Plans for future employment* would be scored as "Not Applicable" for a person who is retired. "See Note" is used for those items that cannot be clearly scored "Independent" or "Needs Assistance" and that require additional explanations. This is only used when there is something unusual about the client's individual circumstances or living situation. When "See

Note" is used, include a short note written to the side of the item on the Score Sheet (see Appendix K for examples). As has been stated previously, it is important that these terms be used for special situations only.

To summarize the results of the evaluation, a final score is computed. Each item marked as "Needs Assistance" is scored as one point, excluding the two items under Work and Leisure. "Needs Assistance" scores under Work and Leisure are counted as only a half ($\frac{1}{2}$) point. "Independent," "See Note," and "Not Applicable" are counted as zero (0). A score of 5 $\frac{1}{2}$ or less indicates the client is capable of living independently. A total score of 6 or more indicates the client needs assistance to live in the community. When a client has a score in the range of 5 - 5 $\frac{1}{2}$, the client has borderline skills for living independently in the community. Further information and evaluations by the occupational therapist and other team members may be needed to make recommendations about living skills and the ability to live in the community. The total score is used by the evaluator to make recommendations, but the total score is not actually recorded on the Score Sheet. The score, however, can be mentioned in the summary note if it helps to clarify the recommendations.

After the final score is computed, a short summary note is written at the bottom of the Score Sheet (see Appendix K for examples). Additional information regarding a person's ability to function is obtained by the evaluator during the administration of the KELS, including the client's orientation, attention span, memory, figure ground, and time management. This information is not scored in the KELS but may be important to include in the summary note. However, the note should always be kept to a minimum and include only highlights and truly meaningful information regarding the ability to perform daily living skills. At the end of the summary note, recommendations for appropriate living situations and further intervention and training needs are made.

In determining the appropriate living situations for clients, many factors must be considered. First, the occupational therapist must examine the items that were scored as "Needs Assistance" and compare them to the assistance available for the client in different types of settings and in the community. The resources for assistance from family members, friends, and neighbors must also be analyzed. If assistance can be provided either by the setting, by individuals, or by agencies, then a person may be able to live safely and competently in a particular environment when the necessary assistance is provided. If a person needs assistance with money management and food, halfway houses generally provide that kind of support and assistance. Nursing facilities provide more care by also supplying assistance in the areas of safety, health, and leisure. Parents, spouses, relatives, and community agencies are also able to supply assistance with living skills, but the amount of assistance available varies greatly from situation to situation.

Two different elderly individuals might score exactly the same on each item, but because of a difference in the availability of supporting resources, the final recommendations might be for one to live alone in the community and for the other to move to an adult foster home. Each case must be examined on an individual basis. If further intervention and/or training is needed, this should also be included in the summary note (see Appendix K for examples).

Morrow (1985) created the Community Support Scale, which is a tool to assist therapists in quantifying the assistance needed to compensate for the living skills for which the client scored "Needs Assistance." It was used as part of the scoring procedure for a research project involving geriatric patients. Study results are discussed in the research section, and the Community Support Scale is included in Appendix J. This scale may be helpful in determining if the assistance available to an individual is adequate for the person to meet the daily living skill demands of the environment. To date, the Community Support Scale has been used only in this one study and needs to be researched further. It is appropriate to use it as a guideline for making recommendations for placement of clients.

Research

S ix research studies completed on the Kohlman Evaluation of Living Skills (KELS) have helped to establish the reliability and validity of the KELS. Relatively small sample sizes (50 or less) were used in all the studies. Research involving larger sample sizes and examining more variables needs to be done to document further the effectiveness of the KELS.

Interrater Reliability Study

Investigators: Ilika and Hoffman

Date: 1981

Location: Minnesota

Population: Psychiatric patients

Description of Study: The exact research design is unknown, and the study was unpublished.

Results: Interrater correlations were significant at $p \leq .001$ with a variance from 74% to 94% agreement.

Discussion: In some of the subsequent studies, minor changes in the administration procedures were made, resulting in higher percentages of reliability.

Concurrent Validity Study

Investigators: Ilika and Hoffman

Date: 1981

Location: Minnesota

Population: Psychiatric treatment setting

Description of Study: Scores from the Kohlman Evaluation of Living Skills and the Global Assessment Scale were compared. The research design is unknown and the study was unpublished.

Results: Correlations of .78 to .89 were found with significance at $p \leq .001$.

Discussion: The results of this study were favorable. Both evaluations test dysfunction in psychiatric patients but evaluate different factors.

Concurrent Validity Study

Investigator: Kaufman

Date: 1982

Location: Florida

Population: Psychiatric inpatients

Description of Study: Psychiatric inpatients were administered the KELS and the Bay Area Functional Performance Evaluation (BaFPE). Results: The scores from the evaluations were compared, and a correlation of $-.84$ ($p \leq .0001$) was established. A negative correlation value occurred because the test scores of the KELS and the BaFPE vary in opposite directions, i.e., a high score on the BaFPE is indicative of greater function, and a high score on the KELS indicates greater dysfunction.

Discussion: Both the KELS and the BaFPE are designed to evaluate function and dysfunction in psychiatric patients, but they examine different factors. The results were positive in helping to establish the validity of the KELS.

Concurrent Validity Study

Investigator: Tateichi

Date: 1984

Location: State of Washington

Population: People living in a halfway house (Congregate Care Facility) and people living independently

Description of Study: The purpose of this study was to test the hypothesis that clients living independently are more likely to have lower scores (greater function) on the KELS than clients living in a sheltered setting. The KELS was administered to 20 people living in a halfway house (CCF) and to 20 people living alone in the community. In the study, Tateichi also examined if the cut-off score of 5 differentiated between the two groups. Unfortunately, an error was made in that the actual cut-off score for independence on the KELS is a score of $5\,^1/_2$, not 5.

Results: The Mann-Whitney U Test was used to compare the KELS scores of the two groups. The results were significant at $p \leq .001$ with U = 47. Consistent with the hypothesis, people who lived alone scored lower on the KELS (indicates more independent) than people living in the sheltered setting.

When the cut-off score of 5 was examined, the results were significant ($p \leq .05$), but a high incidence of false negatives occurred. In this study, a false negative was a person who scored more independent in living skills than the setting required—that is, a person scoring $5\,^1/_2$ or greater and living in a halfway house.

In the analysis of the scores of the two groups, 45% of the clients living in the sheltered setting scored greater than 6, meaning they were accurately identified as needing a setting that provided assistance with living skills.

Fifty-five percent (55%) scored less than 5, which indicated the ability to live alone in the community. In the subjects that were living alone, 90% scored less than 5 (accurately identified by the KELS) and 10% scored greater than 6.

Interrater reliability was established on three consecutive trials prior to the testing. The percentages of agreement were 84%, 94%, and 94%.

Discussion: The results were viewed as positive in demonstrating an expected difference in daily living skills between the two groups. As was mentioned previously, it was unfortunate the actual cut-off score was not used in the study. The issue of a high incidence of false negatives is not of particular concern to the author because of the many reasons people choose to live in halfway houses. It cannot be assumed that just because a person lives in a halfway house he or she does not have the ability to perform the daily living skills necessary to live independently. The subjects that were of greater concern were the 10% who scored greater than 6 and were living alone in the community. The KELS would have recommended that this group live in a sheltered type setting or receive support and assistance to live in the community. It would be important to analyze this group in terms of what kind of assistance the clients were receiving, how long each client had been living alone, whether each client would have still been living alone 4 to 6 months later, and what the hospitalization rate was. This type of additional information would provide valuable direction in determining if items in the KELS need to be revised in order to increase the test's validity.

The interrater reliability was in the acceptable to high range. The evaluator in the study was not an occupational therapist but was able to establish high interrater reliability with very few trials and training in the administration procedures.

Predictive Validity Study

Investigator: Morrow

Date: 1985

Location: State of Washington

Population: Inpatients on a geriatric unit

Description of Study: Twenty inpatients on a geriatric unit were administered the KELS prior to discharge. Forty to 60 days after hospital discharge the predischarge KELS scores were compared to the actual living situations of the subjects. The purpose of the study was to determine if the KELS could accurately predict placement. Of the 20 subjects, 13 were discharged to community living and 7 were discharged to nursing homes. As part of the study, Morrow developed a Community Support Scale (see Appendix J) as a supplemental scoring scale to the KELS. For each living skill item in the KELS, the Community Support Scale gave the specific type of assistance the patient would need to remain in the community. If an item was scored as "Needs Assistance," the Community Support Scale was used to determine if the person would have adequate support and assistance to live in a particular setting. If it was determined that adequate support and assistance were available for an item, the KELS Score for the item was changed to a zero, thus lowering the total KELS Score and giving the person a new adjusted KELS Score.

Results: Forty to 60 days postdischarge, both the KELS and the adjusted KELS Scores were 100% accurate in predicting which of the geriatric subjects would be successful in community placements. In the group that scored greater than $5 \frac{1}{2}$ and had been recommended by the investigator for nursing home placement, 50% were actually living in the community. With the use of the Community Support Scale and the adjusted KELS scores, the positive predictive value for this group improved to 72%.

Prior to the study on two consecutive trials, interrater reliability was calculated. On both the KELS and the adjusted KELS scores 100% agreement was achieved. The administration procedures described in this present edition of the KELS were used for the study.

Discussion: In this study, one problem occurred with the interpretation of the KELS score: nursing home placement was recommended for all patients scoring greater than $5 \frac{1}{2}$. In the scoring procedures of the KELS, however, a score greater than $5 \frac{1}{2}$ indicates only that the client would need assistance to live in the community. For people with scores greater than $5 \frac{1}{2}$, the evaluator might determine that a person needs nursing home placement, but this should not be an automatic recommendation.

The Community Support Scale provided a systematic method to assist in making recommendations for placement following the administration and scoring of the KELS. With further research on the validity of this tool, it could be valuable in quantifying the assistance needed by clients to live in the community. It is included in Appendix J for use as a guideline in making recommendations for appropriate living situations.

Predictive Validity Study

Investigator: McGourty (now Thomson)

Date: 1987

Location: State of Washington

Population: Psychiatric inpatients

Description of Study: Funding for this study was provided by a grant from the American Occupational Therapy Foundation. The purpose of the study was to analyze whether the KELS could accurately predict successful independent living after discharge from an inpatient psychiatric unit. The subjects were 50 psychiatric inpatients who had been discharged to live alone in the community. While they were in the hospital, each subject was administered the KELS, but the results were not given to the treatment team that made the disposition plans. A follow-up contact was made 40 to 60 days after discharge to determine if the subjects were still living independently.

Results: Unfortunately, the research design had several major problems which were not detected until after data collection. It would have been desirable to have had more patients with KELS scores greater than $5 \frac{1}{2}$ in order to help determine the accuracy of the KELS in predicting successful independent living. Unfortunately, only 2 patients of the 50 discharged to live alone scored greater than $5 \frac{1}{2}$ and were predicted not to have the necessary living skills to live alone. Forty-four scored $5 \frac{1}{2}$ or less and were predicted to live alone successfully, and 4 patients were unable to be located after discharge.

Another problem occurred because the staff responsible for making the disposition plans for the subjects had been using the KELS to assist with discharge planning for over two years. To their credit, the occupational therapists had effectively trained the staff in the awareness of the critical factors for successful independent living. Even without the KELS for additional information, the staff did an excellent job in discharging patients who would have scored $5 \frac{1}{2}$ or greater on the KELS to live alone in the community. This contributed to the extreme variance that occurred in the size of the two groups. In retrospect, the study may have been more successful if it had been conducted in a setting in which the staff were not familiar with the KELS.

In the follow-up contact 40 to 60 days after discharge, it was found that 19 patients were not living alone. Because only a yes-no response (living alone or not) was analyzed, the study did not have a method to determine if the patient was not living alone due to a failure to perform living skills or because of some other valid reason—such as going into a residential mental health program or having roommates move in. Either of these reasons may have had nothing to do with a failure to perform living skills and may actually have been an indication of an ability to manage money and to problem solve (i.e., living expenses would be reduced with a roommate).

Interrater reliability was 98% of agreement determined with ongoing reliability checks during data collection. The administration procedures found in this edition of the KELS were used for this study.

Discussion: Interrater reliability was very high and positive, but the validity results of the study were disappointing. It is felt by the author that this occurred because of the many limitations in the research design. It would be helpful if this study could be replicated with the identified problems eliminated.

Applications and Limitations

The Kohlman Evaluation of Living Skills provides valuable information for determining a person's ability to function in basic living skills. It can be used with many populations and in many settings. Although it was originally developed for use in a short-term inpatient psychiatric unit, it is a helpful assessment tool with other populations and settings, including (a) the elderly in nursing facilities, inpatient units, and outpatient settings; (b) acute care units in hospitals; (c) people with brain injuries; and (d) adolescents in training programs. It is an appropriate assessment tool for quickly obtaining information regarding the ability of a person to perform basic living skills.

The KELS, used throughout the United States and in Canada, is based on the urban lifestyles and culture found in the United States. When it is used in rural areas some items must be scored "Not Applicable." It is important to consider where the particular client lives, because that location may have different living skill demands than where the KELS is administered.

If a patient has been hospitalized for longer than one month, the KELS should be used cautiously. After being hospitalized for longer than one month, a person's living situation changes—sometimes dramatically. Frequently someone will be assisting the patient with paying bills; budgeting needs are different; and the patient has been unable to participate in his or her usual work and leisure activities. When giving the KELS in these situations, the knowledge of living skills is usually tested for conditions applicable prior to the hospitalization. The KELS is still a valuable tool for obtaining information in these cases, but the administration of additional living skill assessments, particularly those involving task performance, is recommended.

In order to keep the administration and scoring of the KELS brief, more of the items are interview-based than task-based and performance-based. This means that some items of the KELS test knowledge rather than the actual performance of the living skills. If the evaluator questions whether the client can actually perform a skill he or she has demonstrated knowledge of, additional performance-based testing should be done to supplement the KELS. Because some living skills are not included in the KELS, it is also recommended that other evaluations be done, when applicable, to assess additional areas, such as ability to function in a kitchen or knowledge of basic nutrition.

The KELS is intended to be a short basic living skills evaluation and is not designed to comprehensively evaluate living skills. During the administration of the KELS, the evaluator may determine that further testing may be needed. This is an appropriate part of the total assessment process and should always be done when questions remain regarding a person's ability to function in a particular area. The KELS is only one tool to be used in the assessment process.

In whatever setting the KELS is used, it is important to educate other professionals about how to interpret and use the results in order to prevent any misinterpretation. A variety of educational methods are effective, such as individual contacts, written materials, and in-services. Periodic reeducation is important in order to insure the proper use and interpretation of the KELS results.

The ideal use of the KELS is in a multidisciplinary team approach with the involvement of the client in the decision making process. The KELS is a valuable tool for determining the best environment for a person to live in that will allow as much independence as possible, but it is rarely, if ever, used as the sole determinant of a person's living situation or disposition.

As with many occupational therapy evaluations that are in the development process, the KELS needs to be further researched in order to continue to establish its reliability and validity. Larger sample sizes need to be used, and studies need to be done on a greater variety of populations. The research completed to date is very encouraging, and the face validity of the KELS is very high. The author hopes that further research on the Kohlman Evaluation of Living Skills will be as promising.

References

Ilika, J., & Hoffman, N. G. (1981). *Concurrent validity study on the Kohlman Evaluation of Living Skills and the Global Assessment Scale.* Unpublished manuscript.

Ilika, J., & Hoffman, N. G. (1981). *Reliability study on the Kohlman Evaluation of Living Skills.* Unpublished manuscript.

Kaufman, L. (1982). *Concurrent validity study on the Kohlman Evaluation of Living Skills and the Bay Area Functional Performance Evaluation.* Unpublished master's thesis, University of Florida, Gainesville.

McGourty, L. K. (1979). *Kohlman Evaluation of Living Skills.* Seattle, WA: KELS Research.

Morrow, M. (1985). *A predictive validity study of the Kohlman Evaluation of Living Skills.* Unpublished master's thesis, University of Washington, Seattle.

Tateichi, S. (1985). *A concurrent validity study of the Kohlman Evaluation of Living Skills.* Unpublished master's thesis, University of Washington, Seattle.

White, R. W. (1959). Motivation reconsidered: The concept of competence. *Psychological Review 66,* 297-333.

Appendices

Appendix A:
Reading and Writing Form

PLEASE FILL IN THE FORM BELOW.

DATE _____

NAME _____

ADDRESS _____

_____

_____

AGE _____

HOW OFTEN DO YOU DO THE FOLLOWING ACTIVITIES?

SHOWER OR BATHE _____

WASH FACE _____

WASH HAIR _____

COMB HAIR _____

BRUSH TEETH _____

EAT _____

Appendix B:
Household Situation Picture #1

Appendix B:
Household Situation Picture #2

Appendix B:
Household Situation Picture #3

Appendix B:
Household Situation Picture #4

Appendix C:
Deck of Cards/Bar of Soap

$1.58

$.23

Appendix D:
Budget Form

HOW MUCH MONEY DO YOU SPEND FOR THE FOLLOWING CATEGORIES EACH MONTH?

RENT   _____

UTILITIES   _____

PHONE   _____

TRANSPORTATION   _____

CLOTHING   _____

LEISURE ACTIVITIES   _____

PERSONAL ITEMS   _____

SAVINGS   _____

FOOD   _____

OTHER   _____

Appendix E:
Checking Account Form

Check No.	Date	Checks drawn or deposits made	Amount of check (−)	Check fee (if any)	Amount of deposit (+)	BALANCE FORWARD
						$46.00

Please be sure to deduct any per check charges or maintenance charges that may apply to your account

1st National Bank   105

NON-NEGOTIABLE
PRACTICE CHECK

_____ 19_____

PAY TO
THE ORDER OF _____ $ _____

_____ DOLLARS

MEMO _____ _____

Appendix F:
Savings Account Form

☐ SEND CASHIER'S CHECK
☐ DEPOSIT TO CHECKING ACCOUNT

DATE _____

CHARGE MY
SAVINGS
ACCOUNT _____ DOLLARS

SAVINGS WITHDRAWAL

AMOUNT WITHDRAWN	
$	

SIGNATURE _____

Appendix G:
Bill

<table>
<tr><td rowspan="3">

CITY
ELECTRIC
COMPANY

</td><td>DUE DATE</td><td>AMOUNT DUE</td></tr>
<tr><td>AUG 04, 95</td><td>43.11</td></tr>
</table>

CITY
ELECTRIC
COMPANY

DUE DATE   AMOUNT DUE

AUG 04, 95   43.11

Please show amount of payment:

ACCT NO: 012 34 5678

$ _____

Please write your account number on your check

Make payable to CITY ELECTRIC COMPANY

Used enclosed envelope or mail to:
CITY ELECTRIC COMPANY, Anytown, ST 99999

If paying in person, please bring entire bill

**MAIL THIS PORTION
WITH PAYMENT**

Previous billing $	44.79
Our records show payment(s) $	44.79-
Leaving a balance of $	.00

SUMMER RATES APPLY **ACCOUNT NUMBER** 012 34 5678

SERVICE		METER NUMBER	METER READING		BILLING ACTIVITY	AMOUNT
FROM	TO		PRESENT	PREVIOUS		
MAY 15	JUL 14	161441	5130	3821	1309 KWH	

```
        SUMMER RATE
            YOUR FIRST       440 KWH AT .0207        9.11
            YOUR NEXT        520 KWH AT .0333       17.31
                                    SUBTOTAL        26.42
        SUMMER RATE
            YOUR FIRST       160 KWH AT .0166        2.66
            YOUR NEXT        189 KWH AT .0333        6.30
                                    SUBTOTAL         8.96        35.38
        MAY 15 JUL 14 STREET LIGHT                                7.73

        TAXES INCLUDED IN YOUR BILL ARE
            $2.34 ELEC — OCCUPATION TAX             6.600%
            $1.36 ELEC — STATE UTILITY TAX          3.852%

        SOMETHING NEW FOR A HOT SUMMER. WE NOW REPAIR REFRIGERATORS/FREEZERS. CALL
        555-2323 AND ASK FOR APPLIANCE SERVICE.
```

AVERAGE DAILY COST ELECTRICITY THIS BILL 0.59	COMPARE YOUR USE		
	DAYS	TOTAL KWH	KWH PER DAY
CURRENT PERIOD	60	1309	22
SAME PERIOD LAST YEAR	60	1269	21

DUE DATE

AUG 04, 95

AMOUNT ➡ DUE

43.11

KEEP THIS PORTION

**FARWEST
TAXI**

**IMAX CINEMAS
555-9990**

KELS Score Sheet

Kohlman Evaluation of Living Skills (KELS)

Independent	Needs Assistance

Self-Care

1. Appearance
2. Frequency of self-care activities (self-report)

Safety and Health

1. Awareness of dangerous household situations (from photographs)
2. Identification of appropriate action for sickness and accidents
3. Knowledge of emergency numbers
4. Knowledge of location of medical and dental facilities

Money Management

1. Use of money in purchasing items
2. Obtain and maintain source of income
3. Budgeting of money for food
4. Budgeting of monthly income
5. Use of banking forms
6. Payment of bills

Transportation and Telephone

1. Mobility within community—Methods:
2. Basic knowledge of transit system
3. Use of phone book and telephone

Work and Leisure

1. Plans for future employment
2. Leisure activity involvement

Appendix J
Community Support Scale

This scale was developed by Morrow as part of a master's thesis research project. It can be used as a guideline to assist in developing recommendations after the administration of the Kohlman Evaluation of Living Skills (KELS). When an item is scored as "Needs Assistance," this scale can help determine the level of assistance that might be needed in order for the client to live in the community.

To use the table, locate the item that was scored "Needs Assistance" under the column on the left. The right column defines the assistance that is needed in order for the living skill to be met for that client. As part of the methodology of the study, the KELS Score was adjusted by using this table. It is premature at this stage of research to use the chart in this manner. The author believes that adjusting the KELS score can be confusing; in the discharge planning process, it could easily be forgotten that the client only has a higher score if the assistance is actually present. Therefore, it is recommended that the KELS score not be adjusted and that the assistance needed be clearly defined in the recommendations. The Community Support Scale can be used to assist in making recommendations for living situations and types of assistance needed.

KELS Item That Is Scored "Needs Assistance"	Assistance That Must Be Provided
Self-Care	
1. Appearance	Discharged to community—living with other(s)
2. Frequency of self-care activities (self-report)	Discharged to community—living with other(s)
Safety and Health	
1. Awareness of dangerous household situations (from photographs)	Discharged to community—living with other(s) and receiving constant supervision
2. Identification of appropriate action for sickness and accidents	Discharged to community—living with other(s) and receiving constant supervision

3. Knowledge of emergency numbers

4. Knowledge of location of medical and dental facilities

Discharged to community—living with other(s) and receiving constant supervision

Transportation provided by someone else

Money Management

1. Use of money in purchasing items

2. Obtain and maintain source of income

3. Budgeting of money for food

4. Budgeting of monthly income

5. Use of banking forms

6. Payment of bills

Shopping done by someone else

Paying bills and banking done by someone else

Budgeting of money for food done by someone else

Budgeting of monthly income done by someone else

Paying bills and banking done by someone else

Paying bills and banking done by someone else

Transportation and Telephone

1. Mobility within the community— Methods:

2. Basic knowledge of transit system

3. Use of phone book and telephone

Transportation provided by someone else

Transportation provided by someone else

Discharged to community—living with other(s)

Work and Leisure

1. Plans for future employment

2. Leisure activity involvement

Not applicable for this population*

Discharged to community—living with other(s)

---

*This scale was developed for use with geriatric inpatients who were preparing for discharge. Therefore, for different populations, the necessary assistance would need to be defined.

Appendix K:
Sample Score Sheet #1

1-8-92 **Kohlman Evaluation of Living Skills (KELS)**

Copyright © 1992 by the American Occupational Therapy Association

Independent	Needs Assistance

Self-Care

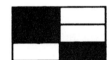

1. Appearance *– in pajamas, hair uncombed – not scored*
2. Frequency of self-care activities (self-report)

Safety and Health

1. Awareness of dangerous household situations (from photographs)
2. Identification of appropriate action for sickness and accidents
3. Knowledge of emergency numbers
4. Knowledge of location of medical and dental facilities

Money Management

Not Applicable

1. Use of money in purchasing items
2. Obtain and maintain source of income
3. Budgeting of money for food
4. Budgeting of monthly income
5. Use of banking forms
6. Payment of bills

Transportation and Telephone

1. Mobility within community—Methods: *Walk & Bus*
2. Basic knowledge of transit system
3. Use of phone book and telephone

Work and Leisure

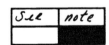

1. Plans for future employment *– has worked, but does not*
2. Leisure activity involvement *plan to work in the future*

Results indicate that client does not have sufficient living skills to return to living in his apt. alone. Therapist recommends a living situation that would manage client's money (half-way house). Training will be reinitiated in future OT sessions for the sections scored Needs Assistance.

Jennifer Jones, OTR

Appendix K:
Sample Score Sheet #2

2-2-92

Kohlman Evaluation of Living Skills (KELS)

Copyright © 1992 by the American Occupational Therapy Association

Independent | Needs Assistance

Self-Care
1. Appearance
2. Frequency of self-care activities (self-report)

Safety and Health
1. Awareness of dangerous household situations (from photographs)
2. Identification of appropriate action for sickness and accidents
3. Knowledge of emergency numbers
4. Knowledge of location of medical and dental facilities

Money Management
1. Use of money in purchasing items
2. Obtain and maintain source of income *husband provides income*
3. Budgeting of money for food
4. Budgeting of monthly income
5. Use of banking forms
6. Payment of bills

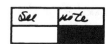

Transportation and Telephone
1. Mobility within community—Methods: *Walker or husband drives*
2. Basic knowledge of transit system
3. Use of phone book and telephone

Work and Leisure

See note

1. Plans for future employment - *has never worked, does not*
2. Leisure activity involvement *plan to work in the future*

Husband provides assistance or does many of basic living skills for Pt. Rx program for future training in living skills will be discussed c̄ Pt. & in family conference. Recommend the life skills Prog. to ↓ Pt's dependence on husband & ↑ confidence & self esteem provided Pt & family agree.

Jennifer Jones, OTR

Appendix K:
Sample Score Sheet #3

3-7-92   **Kohlman Evaluation of Living Skills (KELS)**

Copyright © 1992 by the American Occupational Therapy Association

Independent | Needs Assistance

Self-Care
1. Appearance
2. Frequency of self-care activities (self-report)

Safety and Health
1. Awareness of dangerous household situations (from photographs)
2. Identification of appropriate action for sickness and accidents
3. Knowledge of emergency numbers
4. Knowledge of location of medical and dental facilities

Money Management
1. Use of money in purchasing items
2. Obtain and maintain source of income
3. Budgeting of money for food
4. Budgeting of monthly income
5. Use of banking forms
6. Payment of bills

Transportation and Telephone
1. Mobility within community—Methods: *has own car*
2. Basic knowledge of transit system
3. Use of phone book and telephone

Work and Leisure
1. Plans for future employment *Plans to return to job*
2. Leisure activity involvement

Client has sufficient living skills to live independently. A referral to the Leisure Group will be made and living skills scored Needs Assistance will be reviewed with OT.

Jennifer Jones, OTR